My 'thinky-thoughts' journal

Created for awesome kids everywhere
by Fi Star-Stone
Copyright © 2020 Fi Star-Stone

All rights reserved.

ISBN: 9798632268479

Written by the Epic Author know as…

(psst put your name here!)_____

My
'thinky-thoughts' journal

My lockdown notes and cool ideas!

ACKNOWLEDGMENTS

Write here all the people you'd like to thank
who helped you during lockdown

It's a nice way of showing people how thankful you are
and how much you care about them.

_____

_____

_____

_____

_____

ii

Introduction

The 2019-20 Coronavirus Pandemic (Covid19) meant that lots of children, just like you, had to stay in their homes. This was called 'Lockdown' and it was to keep everyone safe from catching or spreading the nasty virus.

Lots of children were homeschooled, lots of children were bored, and lots of children had worrying feelings and thoughts that were helped by writing things down.

It wasn't all doom and gloom though! There was also lots of fun and there was a lot of kindness in the world.

This journal is for you to write down all of your 'thinky-thoughts' to log the story of your life during the Covid19 pandemic 2019/20.

All about me!

My name is...	
My age is...	
The country I live in is...	
I live with...	
My hobbies are...	
My favourite food is...	

This is me!

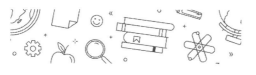 Today's date

_____

Today, in my own words, 'I am feeling'

_____

_____

_____

One rubbish thing about today

_____

Three AWESOME things about today

1. _____

2. _____

3. _____

An interesting thing I learned today was...

_____

People I spoke to today (in real life, online, or on the phone!)

The yummiest food I ate today was...

_____

I'm looking forward to...

_____

My doodle space

Doodling is really good for your brain,
Draw sunshine and rainbows, or umbrellas and rain!
How about a monster that's friendly and kind?
Doodle whatever comes into your mind!

My happy space

'When you have an anxious feeling in your tummy, always think of something funny!'

Jokes are really great for taking your mind off things that are worrying you!

Write some funny jokes in the speech bubbles then share them with your friends! or family!

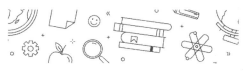 Today's date

_____

Today, in my own words, 'I am feeling'

_____

_____

_____

One rubbish thing about today

_____

Three AWESOME things about today

1. _____

2. _____

3. _____

An interesting thing I learned today was...

_____

People I spoke to today (in real life, online, or on the phone!)

The yummiest food I ate today was...

_____

I'm looking forward to...

_____

Weird, cool, kind and crazy stuff during the pandemic

During the lockdown, lots of very unusual things happened! Can you write a few of the things down?

For example - what happened to school life? What about the supermarkets? And what about toilet roll shortages? Were people kind? Helpful? How did people stay in touch?

_____

_____

_____

_____

_____

Covid 19 in the news

On the TV, in newspapers and on social media, you may have seen or heard lots of worrying stories.

On the next page, draw a picture or stick a newspaper article in the next page to show life during the worldwide pandemic.

It can be a happy news story, or maybe a headline announcing the lockdown. Ask a grown-up to help you find something to stick in or copy and draw.

You could also write your own news story! pretend you are a reporter and write a headline and story on the next page.

Covid 19 in the news

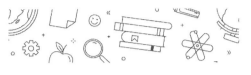 Today's date

_____

Today, in my own words, 'I am feeling'

_____

_____

_____

One rubbish thing about today

_____

Three AWESOME things about today

1. _____

2. _____

3. _____

An interesting thing I learned today was...

_____

People I spoke to today (in real life, online, or on the phone!)

The yummiest food I ate today was...

_____

I'm looking forward to...

_____

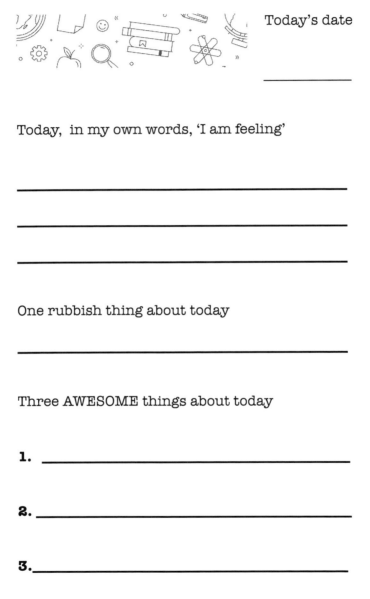

Today's date

_____

Today, in my own words, 'I am feeling'

_____

_____

_____

One rubbish thing about today

_____

Three AWESOME things about today

1. _____

2. _____

3. _____

An interesting thing I learned today was...

_____

People I spoke to today (in real life, online, or on the phone!)

The yummiest food I ate today was...

_____

I'm looking forward to...

_____

My lockdown invention

Lockdown may seem scary and rather boring but did you know some pretty awesome discoveries were made during social distancing in history?

In 1665, governments, schools and many businesses closed and the government imposed 'social distancing' just like todays pandemic. Cambridge University sent students home to continue their studies.

Isaac Newton was one of those students and spent his time wisely. He focused on mathematical problems and experiments and on returning to Cambridge in 1667, theories in hand he was made a fellow! Two years later, he was a professor!

So now you're homeschooling over the next few weeks, think of the example Isaac Newton set. Having time to study uninterrupted and experiment in his own home proved life-changing for him!

My lockdown invention

What do you like? What do you really enjoy doing?

Maybe you're into science? Or perhaps you love football? Maybe art is your thing - or maybe you're a brilliant gamer?

Think about something you really love to do - and just like Isaac Newton - really focus on that favourite thing. Practice and research it a little each day and as the weeks mount up - you'll become an 'expert' in the thing you love! Set yourself a task or challenge with your favourite thing in mind and a date to have completed it by. give yourself a few weeks and practice lots.

With your favourite thing in mind, create an invention that could change the way you play/work/create or draw, and write about it on the next page. Remember to put lots of detail into your invention idea. Write about the materials you'd use, how much it might cost to fund the invention, who it might help, and how it would work.

You never know - you might be the next Isaac Newton or Grace Hopper!

My lockdown invention

I have based my invention on my favourite thing which is...

_____

_____

About my invention

_____

_____

_____

_____

Who my invention might help

Things needed to make my invention

_____

_____

_____

_____

How much it might cost to fund my invention

A picture of my invention

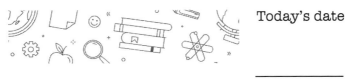

Today's date

_____

Today, in my own words, 'I am feeling'

_____

_____

_____

One rubbish thing about today

_____

Three AWESOME things about today

1. _____

2. _____

3. _____

An interesting thing I learned today was...

_____

People I spoke to today (in real life, online, or on the phone!)

The yummiest food I ate today was...

_____

I'm looking forward to...

_____

My Doodle Space

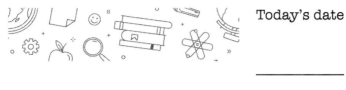

Today's date

_____

Today, in my own words, 'I am feeling'

_____

_____

_____

One rubbish thing about today

_____

Three AWESOME things about today

1. _____

2. _____

3. _____

An interesting thing I learned today was...

_____

People I spoke to today (in real life, online, or on the phone!)

The yummiest food I ate today was...

_____

I'm looking forward to...

_____

Today I'm thankful for...

Sometimes, when things feel a bit overwhelming and out of control, it's easy to get swept up in negativity and feeling really low about the situation.

One thing you can do, is to write down all of the things that make you happy and what you are thankful for. It could be as simple as 'I had my favourite dinner with my family' or 'the sunny day meant I got to play outside!'

Try and think about the non-materialistic things such as good friends and family when you write your list.

There's no right or wrong answer here - it's your 'thankful list' to look back on anytime you feel a bit sad.

Today I'm thankful for...

I'm thankful for...	It makes me feel...

Rainbows around the world

'Try to be a rainbow in someone's cloud!'

Maya Angelou

In hard times, it is important to look for the positives. Some might even say to 'look through the storm for rainbows!'

You may have seen in the news that children all over the world during lockdown, have been drawing, colouring, chalking and painting rainbows and putting them in their windows to keep everyone smiling and positive.

If you'd like to join in with this - ask a grown-up to take your picture with your rainbow and stick it on the next page.

My Rainbow

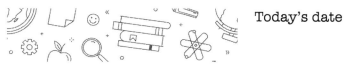

Today's date

_____

Today, in my own words, 'I am feeling'

_____

_____

_____

One rubbish thing about today

_____

Three AWESOME things about today

1. _____

2. _____

3. _____

An interesting thing I learned today was...

_____

People I spoke to today (in real life, online, or on the phone!)

The yummiest food I ate today was...

_____

I'm looking forward to...

_____

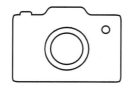 **My lockdown pictures**

Over the next few pages you can either stick a photos or draw your own mini-pictures in the polaroid frames. Describe each drawing or photo underneath.

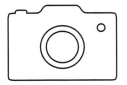 **My lockdown pictures**

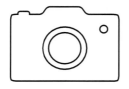 **My lockdown pictures**

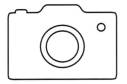 **My lockdown pictures**

A special 'lockdown' memory

What's your loveliest memory from lockdown so far?

_____

_____

_____

_____

_____

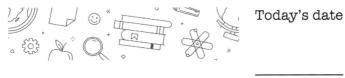 Today's date

_____

Today, in my own words, 'I am feeling'

_____

_____

_____

One rubbish thing about today

_____

Three AWESOME things about today

1. _____

2. _____

3. _____

An interesting thing I learned today was...

_____

People I spoke to today (in real life, online, or on the phone!)

The yummiest food I ate today was...

_____

I'm looking forward to...

_____

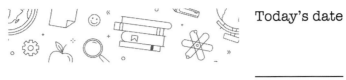

Today's date

_____

Today, in my own words, 'I am feeling'

_____

_____

_____

One rubbish thing about today

_____

Three AWESOME things about today

1. _____

2. _____

3. _____

An interesting thing I learned today was...

_____

People I spoke to today (in real life, online, or on the phone!)

The yummiest food I ate today was...

_____

I'm looking forward to...

_____

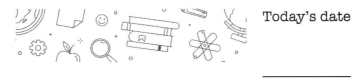

Today's date

_____

Today, in my own words, 'I am feeling'

_____

_____

_____

One rubbish thing about today

_____

Three AWESOME things about today

1. _____

2. _____

3. _____

An interesting thing I learned today was...

_____

People I spoke to today (in real life, online, or on the phone!)

The yummiest food I ate today was...

_____

I'm looking forward to...

_____

Things that have made me sad during lockdown

It's O.K to feel sad sometimes, especially in times of uncertainty when everything feels a little weird.

Lots of grown-ups are feeling sad and worried too at times.

It really helps to jot down those worries to take them out of your head. Sometimes - it can really help to write them on pieces of paper and then throw the worries in the bin!

Perhaps not seeing your friends and family is making you sad? Perhaps not being able to go to your favourite place or club like gymnastics, swimming or football, is really frustrating you and making you feel cross.

Write down your worries or things that have made you sad or cross during lockdown. you won't get into any trouble for being honest! A grown-up will be able to help you with these feelings - so don't be afraid to show them how you are feeling.

The positive thing about writing down these feelings, is when you read them back once lockdown is over, you'll be so thankful for all the things you're allowed to do again!

Things that have made me sad during lockdown

_____

_____

_____

_____

_____

_____

My doodle space

Doodling is really fun,
 Draw a rainbow or the sun!
  Can you draw your family?
   Or maybe what you had for tea!

Wash your hands! (with soap!)

Grown-ups probably tell you this a thousand times a day right?

It's probably really annoying you - but do you know why they keep reminding you to? This may help you to understand the importance of hand washing with soap!

Germ experiment

Ask a grown-up to help you!

Here's a little experiment for you to try - it really is good at explaining why using soap and washing your hands is important in killing the virus from your hands.

You'll need:

- A large bowl
- Pepper
- water
- Liquid soap or washing up liquid

How to:

1.   Fill the bowl with cold water

2. Sprinkle lots of pepper on top (The pepper represents the virus!)

3. Put the tip of your finger into the water - what happens? Does the pepper stick to your finger? This is how germs cling to your fingers and hands!

4. Now put a bit of liquid soap on your finger tip and dip your finger into the water! what happens?

Does the pepper separate in the water? This is how germs react to soap - it kills the virus on your hands! This is why you should always use warm water and soap whenever you wash your hands and wash them for as long as it takes you to sing 'Happy birthday' twice!

What did you think of the experiment? Did you expect that to happen?

_____

_____

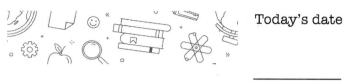

Today's date

_____

Today, in my own words, 'I am feeling'

_____

_____

_____

One rubbish thing about today

_____

Three AWESOME things about today

1. _____

2. _____

3. _____

An interesting thing I learned today was…

_____

People I spoke to today (in real life, online, or on the phone!)

The yummiest food I ate today was…

_____

I'm looking forward to…

_____

 **Lockdown colouring**

Did you know that colouring is good for you?

It's true! Colouring has the ability to relax the 'fear centre' of your brain? (It's called 'the amygdala.')

Colouring induces the same state as meditating by reducing the thoughts of a restless mind. How very smart is that?

With this in mind - why not spend a relaxing half-hour colouring the next couple of pages.

Use pencil crayons rather than felt tips as they may go through the page!

You can doodle around the pictures or add words to them too if you like!

Lockdown colouring

Lockdown colouring

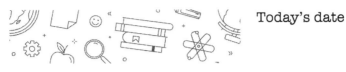

Today's date

_____

Today, in my own words, 'I am feeling'

_____

_____

_____

One rubbish thing about today

_____

Three AWESOME things about today

1. _____

2. _____

3. _____

An interesting thing I learned today was...

_____

People I spoke to today (in real life, online, or on the phone!)

The yummiest food I ate today was...

_____

I'm looking forward to...

_____

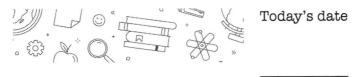 Today's date

_____

Today, in my own words, 'I am feeling'

_____

_____

_____

One rubbish thing about today

_____

Three AWESOME things about today

1. _____

2. _____

3. _____

An interesting thing I learned today was...

_____

People I spoke to today (in real life, online, or on the phone!)

The yummiest food I ate today was...

_____

I'm looking forward to...

_____

Things that have made me happy during lockdown

Sometimes, out of a negative situation - some really positive and happy things happen!

Perhaps you're getting to spend more time eating meals together as a family or playing games you didn't have time to before? Maybe you love homeschooling?

Write down all the things that have made you happy during lockdown. Then, when you read them back once lockdown is over, you'll look back with fondness on these happy moments.

_____

_____

_____

_____

Things that have made me happy during lockdown

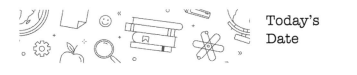

Today's Date

_____

Today, in my own words, 'I am feeling'

_____

_____

_____

One rubbish thing about today

_____

Three AWESOME things about today

1. _____

2. _____

3. _____

An interesting thing I learned today was...

_____

People I spoke to today (in real life, online, or on the phone!)

The yummiest food I ate today was...

_____

I'm looking forward to...

_____

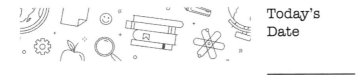

Today's Date
_____

Today, in my own words, 'I am feeling'

_____

_____

_____

One rubbish thing about today

_____

Three AWESOME things about today

1. _____

2. _____

3. _____

An interesting thing I learned today was...

_____

People I spoke to today (in real life, online, or on the phone!)

The yummiest food I ate today was...

_____

I'm looking forward to...

_____

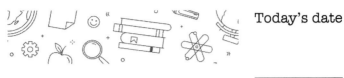 Today's date

_____

Today, in my own words, 'I am feeling'

_____

_____

_____

One rubbish thing about today

_____

Three AWESOME things about today

1. _____

2. _____

3. _____

An interesting thing I learned today was...

_____

People I spoke to today (in real life, online, or on the phone!)

The yummiest food I ate today was...

_____

I'm looking forward to...

_____

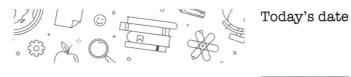

Today's date

_____

Today, in my own words, 'I am feeling'

_____

_____

_____

One rubbish thing about today

_____

Three AWESOME things about today

1. _____

2. _____

3. _____

An interesting thing I learned today was...

_____

People I spoke to today (in real life, online, or on the phone!)

The yummiest food I ate today was...

_____

I'm looking forward to...

_____

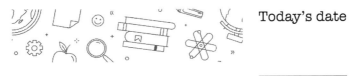 Today's date

_____

Today, in my own words, 'I am feeling'

_____

_____

_____

One rubbish thing about today

_____

Three AWESOME things about today

1. _____

2. _____

3. _____

An interesting thing I learned today was...

_____

People I spoke to today (in real life, online, or on the phone!)

The yummiest food I ate today was...

_____

I'm looking forward to...

_____

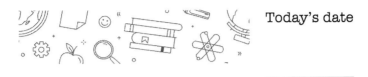

Today's date

_____

Today, in my own words, 'I am feeling'

_____

_____

_____

One rubbish thing about today

_____

Three AWESOME things about today

1. _____

2. _____

3. _____

An interesting thing I learned today was...

_____

People I spoke to today (in real life, online, or on the phone!)

The yummiest food I ate today was...

_____

I'm looking forward to...

_____

My doodle space

Doodling is really great!
whether you're 9 or 58!
Can you draw how you feel today?
Are you 'bah' or 'hip-hip-hooray!'

Homeschooling memories

Have you been homeschooled? Maybe you've always been homeschooled but it's felt a little different during the lockdown?

Write down your happiest, most fun or most interesting lessons you have learned at home.

_____

_____

_____

_____

_____

Homeschooling photos

Stick some photos of your homeschooling days here to look back on.

Today's date

_____

Today, in my own words, 'I am feeling'

_____

_____

_____

One rubbish thing about today

_____

Three AWESOME things about today

1. _____

2. _____

3. _____

An interesting thing I learned today was...

_____

People I spoke to today (in real life, online, or on the phone!)

The yummiest food I ate today was...

_____

I'm looking forward to...

_____

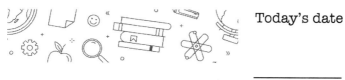 Today's date

_____

Today, in my own words, 'I am feeling'

_____

_____

_____

One rubbish thing about today

_____

Three AWESOME things about today

1. _____

2. _____

3. _____

An interesting thing I learned today was...

_____

People I spoke to today (in real life, online, or on the phone!)

The yummiest food I ate today was...

_____

I'm looking forward to...

_____

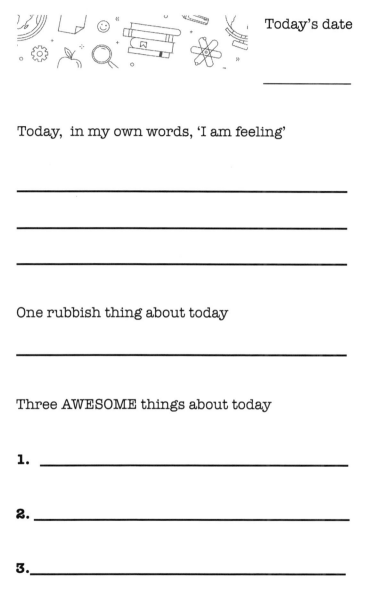

Today's date

_____

Today, in my own words, 'I am feeling'

_____

_____

_____

One rubbish thing about today

_____

Three AWESOME things about today

1. _____

2. _____

3. _____

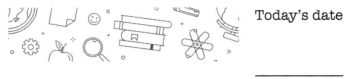

Today's date

_____

Today, in my own words, 'I am feeling'

_____

_____

_____

One rubbish thing about today

_____

Three AWESOME things about today

1. _____

2. _____

3. _____

An interesting thing I learned today was...

_____

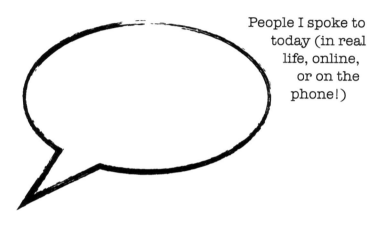

People I spoke to today (in real life, online, or on the phone!)

The yummiest food I ate today was...

_____

I'm looking forward to...

_____

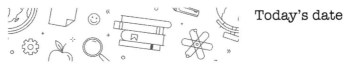 Today's date

_____

Today, in my own words, 'I am feeling'

_____

_____

_____

One rubbish thing about today

_____

Three AWESOME things about today

1. _____

2. _____

3. _____

An interesting thing I learned today was...

___

People I spoke to today (in real life, online, or on the phone!)

The yummiest food I ate today was...

___

I'm looking forward to...

___

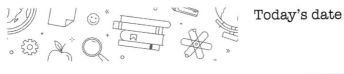

Today's date

_____

Today, in my own words, 'I am feeling'

_____

_____

_____

One rubbish thing about today

_____

Three AWESOME things about today

1. _____

2. _____

3. _____

An interesting thing I learned today was…

_____

People I spoke to today (in real life, online, or on the phone!)

The yummiest food I ate today was…

_____

I'm looking forward to…

_____

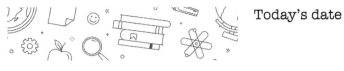

Today's date
_____

Today, in my own words, 'I am feeling'

_____

_____

_____

One rubbish thing about today

_____

Three AWESOME things about today

1. _____

2. _____

3. _____

An interesting thing I learned today was...

_____

People I spoke to today (in real life, online, or on the phone!)

The yummiest food I ate today was...

_____

I'm looking forward to...

_____

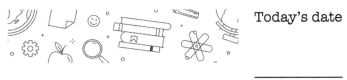 Today's date

_____

Today, in my own words, 'I am feeling'

_____

_____

_____

One rubbish thing about today

_____

Three AWESOME things about today

1. _____

2. _____

3. _____

An interesting thing I learned today was...

_____

People I spoke to today (in real life, online, or on the phone!)

The yummiest food I ate today was...

_____

I'm looking forward to...

_____

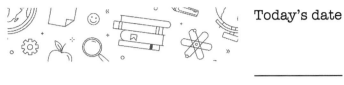

Today's date

_____

Today, in my own words, 'I am feeling'

_____

_____

_____

One rubbish thing about today

_____

Three AWESOME things about today

1. _____

2. _____

3. _____

An interesting thing I learned today was...

_____

People I spoke to today (in real life, online, or on the phone!)

The yummiest food I ate today was...

_____

I'm looking forward to...

_____

My doodle space

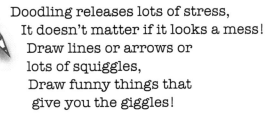

Doodling releases lots of stress,
  It doesn't matter if it looks a mess!
  Draw lines or arrows or
  lots of squiggles,
    Draw funny things that
    give you the giggles!

Final thinky-thoughts

Use the final pages of your journal as the ending to your lockdown story.

Write down any final feelings or anything you might have missed.

What you have learned during the Covid19 pandemic and what are your thoughts about the future?

Will the time you have spent in lockdown at home make you behave differently in future? Do you think things will go back to normal or will they be different in a good way?

Will people be kinder to one another? Maybe you'll carry on spending more time together as a family or you've learned a new hobby while you've been at home?

My final thinky-thoughts

by

_____

_____

_____

_____

_____

_____

95

97

This was the covid19 pandemic lockdown journal of...

_____

Age _____

My best lockdown memory was...

_____

Worst lockdown memory was...

_____

I hope you enjoyed reading my journal.

THE END

Printed in Great Britain
by Amazon